I'M GLAD THERE ARE...

Clouds and Rain

By **Tracey Turner** Illustrated by **Fiona Powers**

WINDMILL BOOKS

Published in 2025 by Windmill Books,
an Imprint of Rosen Publishing
2544 Clinton St.
Buffalo, NY 14224

First published in Great Britain in 2022 by The Watts Publishing Group

Credits
Design and project management: Raspberry Books
Art Direction: Sidonie Beresford-Browne
Design: Kathryn Davies
Illustration: Fiona Powers

Cataloging-in-Publication Data

Names: Turner, Tracey, author. | Powers, Fiona, illustrator.
Title: Clouds and rain / by Tracey Turner, illustrated by Fiona Powers.
Description: Buffalo, New York : Windmill Books, 2025. | Series: I'm glad there are... | Includes glossary and index.
Identifiers: ISBN 9781538396315 (pbk.) | ISBN 9781538396322 (library bound) | ISBN 9781538396339 (ebook)
Subjects: LCSH: Clouds--Juvenile literature. | Rain and rainfall--Juvenile literature. | Weather--Juvenile literature.
Classification: LCC QC921.35 T87 2025 | DDC 551.57'6--dc23

Printed in the United States of America
CPSIA Compliance Information: Batch #CSWM25: For Further Information contact Rosen Publishing at 1-800-237-9932

I'M GLAD THERE ARE...

Clouds and Rain

By **Tracey Turner**

Illustrated by **Fiona Powers**

WINDMILL BOOKS™

Contents

6 Clouds and Rain

8 Different Types of Clouds

10 Fluffy Clouds

12 Rain

14 Rainbows

16 Sunshine

18 The World Recycles Water

20 Snow

22 Frost

24 Thunderstorms

26 Misty Mornings

28 Seasons

30 Glossary

32 Index

I'M GLAD THERE ARE

Clouds and Rain

I LOVE CLOUDS AND RAIN! They're the reason the world is full of green plants and flowers.

- Clouds make amazing shapes that are fun to spot.
- Splashing in rainy puddles is fun!

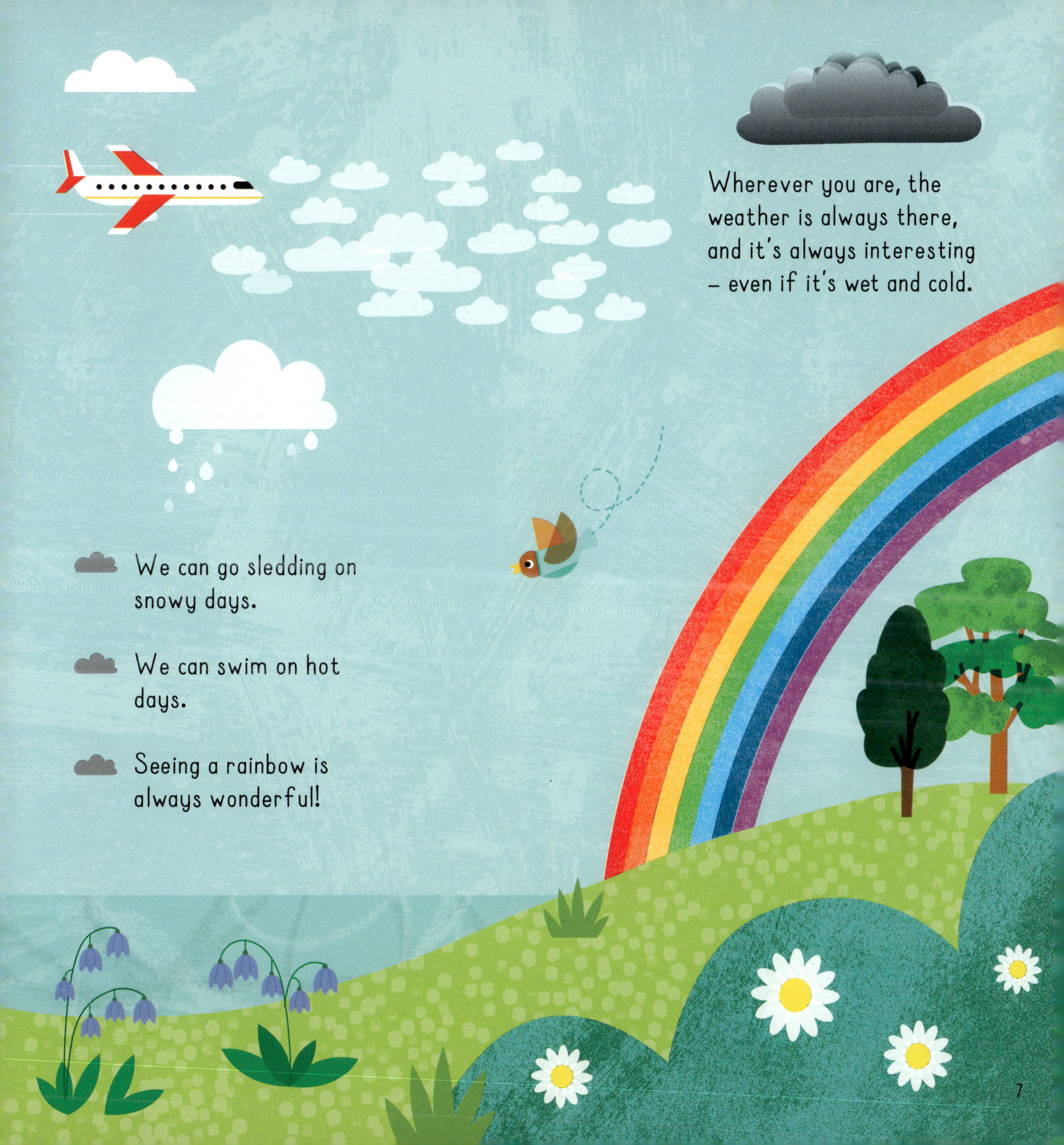

Wherever you are, the weather is always there, and it's always interesting – even if it's wet and cold.

- We can go sledding on snowy days.
- We can swim on hot days.
- Seeing a rainbow is always wonderful!

I'M GLAD THERE ARE

Different Types of Clouds

...because they help predict the weather.

There are lots of DIFFERENT KINDS of CLOUDS:

CIRROSTRATUS CLOUDS are a thin layer of high, white clouds. The sun shines hazily through these clouds.

CIRROCUMULUS CLOUDS are made of ice crystals very high in the sky, and make a beautiful mottled pattern.

Thick, gray clouds covering the whole sky are called **NIMBOSTRATUS** clouds. They often brings heavy rain or snow.

There are many other different types!

I'M GLAD THERE ARE

Fluffy Clouds

...because I like watching the shapes they make.

WHITE, FLUFFY CLOUDS are called cumulus clouds. If you watch them for a while, you might spot shapes. This one looks like a dog!

On a sunny day you might see lots of fluffy clouds. They don't usually hang around for long – new clouds appear, others disappear, and they change shape and size. My dog could change into a rabbit!

Cumulus clouds form when a patch of ground heats up in the sun, making a bubble of warm, damp air that drifts up to make a cloud.

Go cloud watching

Wait for a fine day and go cloud watching. Find somewhere comfy to lie on your back and look up. Draw some of the shapes you see.

I'M GLAD THERE IS

Rain

...because it keeps the world green.

When the tiny drops of water inside clouds become too big, they fall as RAIN.

Plants need water to survive. So if there wasn't any rain, there wouldn't be any green plants in the world. And there wouldn't be any animals that eat the green plants, and the animals that eat them . . . and there wouldn't be any people!

There are different kinds of rain. Drizzle falls from thin clouds in tiny drops. Much bigger drops, which fall from thick, gray clouds, can drench you in a heavy shower.

Make a splash

Another great thing about rain is that it makes puddles! Put on a pair of waterproof boots and jump in a puddle!

I'M GLAD THERE ARE

Rainbows

...because they're a magical surprise on rainy days.

Light is made up of lots of different colors. If light from the sun passes through a drop of water and bounces off the opposite side of the drop, it splits into the colors we see as a RAINBOW.

Rainbows appear when the sun is shining and it's raining at the same time. To look for a rainbow, stand with your back to the sun.

Make a rainbow

Create your own rainbow – stand outside with the sun behind you on a sunny day and spray a hose or watering can so that the water cascades in front of you. A rainbow should appear. You could water plants at the same time!

I'M GLAD THERE IS

Sunshine

...because the whole world needs it.

On a SUNNY DAY, the world seems to sparkle. I love watching sunlight reflecting on a lake, or making dappled shadows as it shines down through trees.

Green plants need lots of sunshine. Instead of eating food, plants get the energy they need from the sun.

The sun keeps the world warm enough for all of the different animals (and us!) to live.

In ancient times, lots of people worshipped the sun. It's easy to see why – the sun brings heat and light, and makes crops grow and ripen for food.

I'M GLAD THE

World Recycles Water

...because it gives us water to drink.

The world is a great big water recycler! Water rises up from the ocean, falls as rain, and then the cycle starts again, giving us water to drink.

1 Water in oceans or lakes is heated by the sun, and changes into water vapor.

2 The water vapor rises and cools and makes clouds. Winds can blow the clouds a long way away from where they formed.

3 When the water droplets in the clouds are big enough, they fall as rain.

4 The rain falls into oceans and lakes and onto the land. Some of the water from the land makes its way into streams, which flow into rivers, which flow into the ocean. And the water cycle begins again!

I'M GLAD THERE IS

Snow

...because it's the weather that is the most fun!

Snow forms inside freezing clouds that contain very tiny crystals of ice. The ice crystals stick together to make SNOWFLAKES. When the flakes are too heavy to stay in the cloud, they fall as snow.

No two snowflakes are the same. If you look at them really closely you'll see amazing and beautiful patterns, like these.

Everything looks different after it's snowed – and it sounds different, too, because snow absorbs sound.

It's fun to roll snowballs and build things with them. Do you like my snow bear?

My absolute favorite is sledding! Whizzing downhill is the best fun ever.

I'M GLAD THERE IS

Frost

...because it makes wintertime sparkle.

When it's really cold, damp air freezes and coats everything with a thin layer of ice crystals – frost!

When damp air freezes quickly, it can make little spiky needles of ice called "hoar frost."

You usually see frost after a clear night in winter. It covers everything it touches in sparkling white, like a layer of glitter. Even ordinary things like cars and lampposts look lovely!

Beautiful frost patterns can form on windows when it's very cold outside. Morning dew on the glass freezes to make ice crystals. The crystals make swirling patterns that look like fern fronds.

I'M GLAD THERE ARE Thunderstorms

...because they're the most dramatic kind of weather.

GREAT BIG THUNDERCLOUDS can grow to 9 miles (15 km) high, or even more. They bring heavy rain, strong winds, flashing lightning, and booming thunder.

Lightning happens when ice crystals and water droplets smash into each other inside a thundercloud. It flashes from the top to the bottom of the cloud, or from the bottom of the cloud to the ground.

Lightning can be dangerous, so stay safe indoors.

Thunder is caused when lightning heats up the air around it, making the air expand really quickly - this makes the loud thunder sound.

I'M GLAD THERE ARE

Misty Mornings

...because they make everything look mysterious.

When the air is damp and the skies are clear, moisture in the air can turn into water droplets near the ground, making mist or fog. Fog is like mist but thicker – sometimes it's really hard to see through it!

Mist clears as the sun warms the air. That's why it's more likely to be misty in the morning, before the sun has warmed things up.

If you live near mountains, you'll see mist gathering in the valleys between them in the morning. This is because cold air flows downhill at night and settles there. It's also common to see mist over rivers, lakes, ponds, and marshy ground.

I'M GLAD THERE ARE

Seasons

...because it's good to have all kinds of weather.

We get **DIFFERENT SEASONS** because the Earth is tilted on its axis.

In the northern half of the world (the Northern Hemisphere), the three warmest months are June, July, and August, when it's summertime. In the Southern Hemisphere, summertime is in December, January, and February.

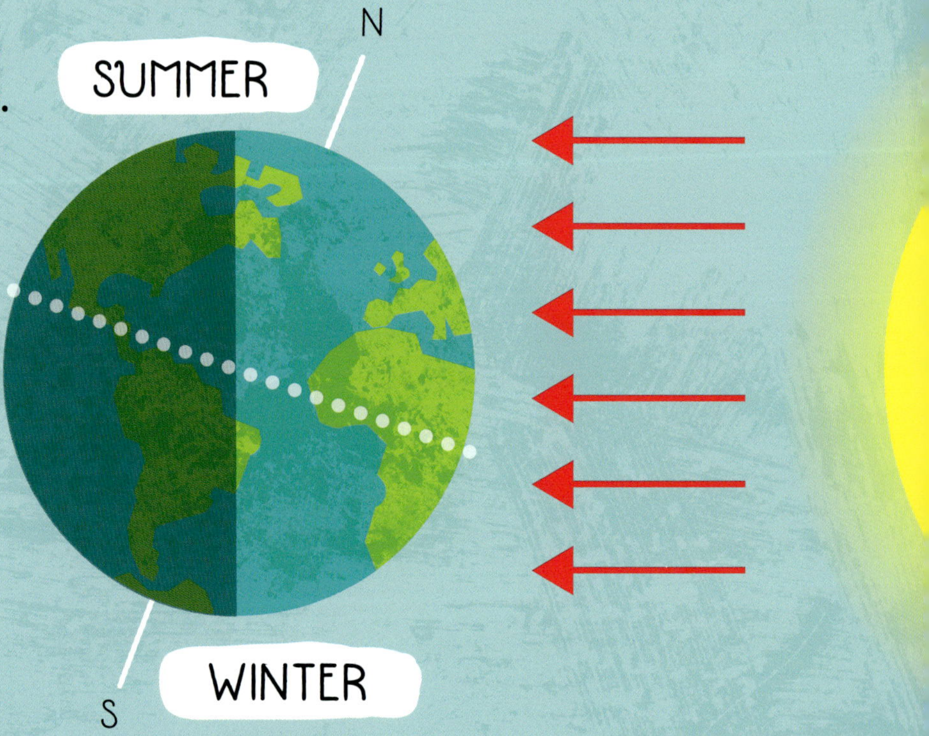

SPRING

Spring is between winter and summer, when the temperature starts to warm up and lots of plants sprout new leaves.

AUTUMN

Autumn is between summer and winter, when it starts to get cooler, and some plants die back for the winter.

SUMMER

The warmest temperatures are in the summer months.

WINTER

The coldest months are December, January, and February in the Northern Hemisphere and June, July, and August in the Southern Hemisphere.

GLOSSARY

Absorbs
soaks up or takes in.

Atmosphere
layer of gases around the Earth, where all weather happens.

Axis
the imaginary line running through Earth from the North Pole to the South Pole around which Earth spins.

Cirrocumulus clouds
high clouds that make a mottled pattern.

Cirrostratus clouds
high-up clouds in a thin layer.

Crops
plants that are grown on farms for food.

Cumulus clouds
white, fluffy clouds.

Current
flow of air or water.

Dew
droplets of water that form outside at night.

Drizzle
tiny drops of rain falling lightly from thin clouds.

Fog
water in tiny droplets near the ground, making it difficult to see far.

Frost
white crystals of ice that form on cold surfaces when damp air freezes.

Hoar frost
frost that freezes quickly to make icy spikes.

Ice
solid water.

Marshy ground
land that is wet, muddy, and soft.

Mist
light fog.

Nimbostratus clouds
thick gray clouds that cover the sky you can see.

Solar
relating to the sun.

Water vapor
water in gas form.

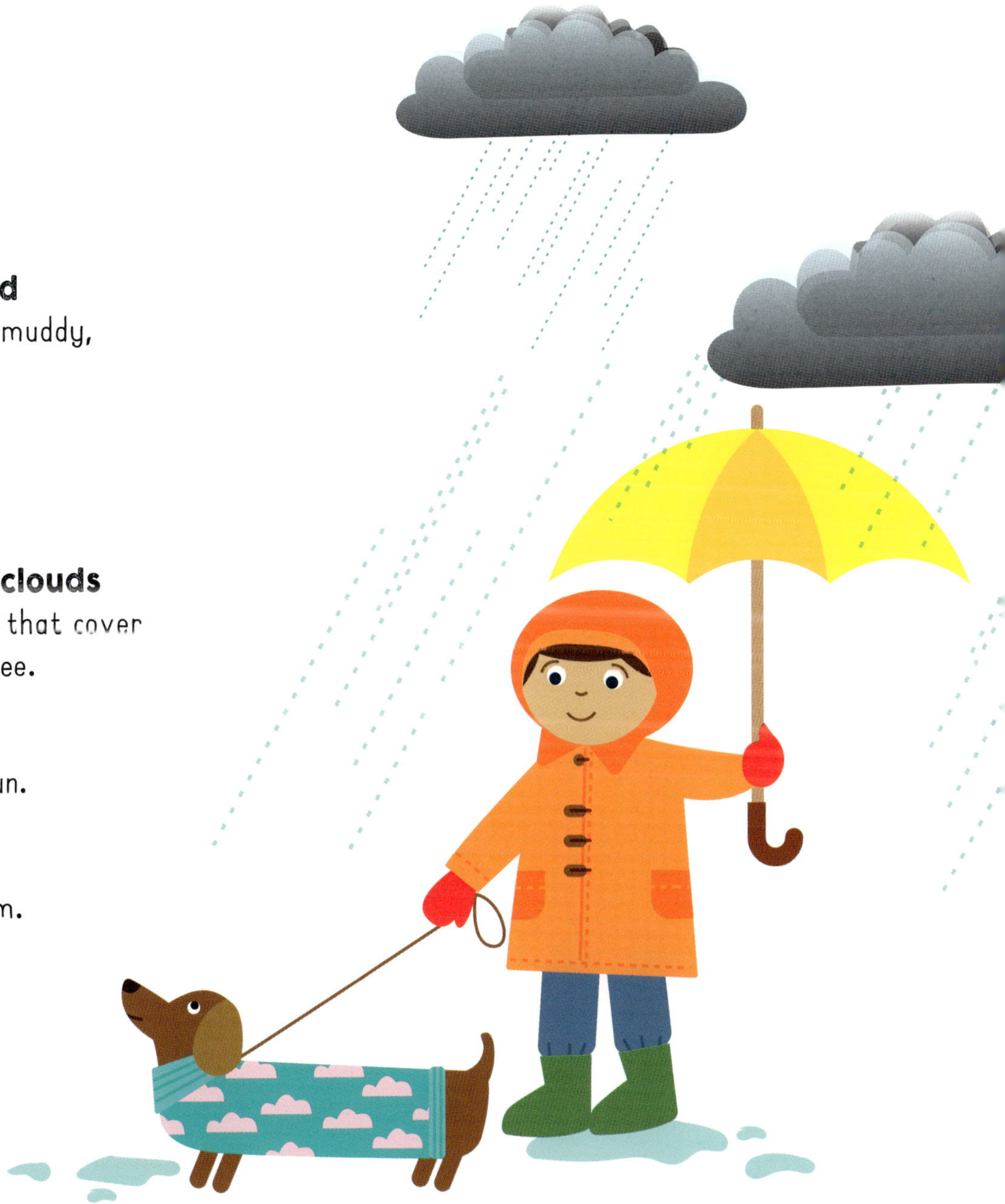

INDEX

autumn 29
axis, Earth's 28, 30

cirrocumulus clouds 8, 30
cirrostratus clouds 8, 30
cloud watching 11
clouds 6, 8–11, 12, 19, 20, 24
crops 17, 30
cumulus clouds 10–11

dew 22, 30
drizzle 12, 30

fluffy clouds 10–11
fog 26, 30
frost 22–23, 30

hoar frost 22, 30

ice crystals 8, 20, 22, 24, 31

lakes and rivers 19, 27
lightning 24, 25

marshy ground 27, 31
mist 26–27, 31

nimbostratus clouds 9, 31
Northern Hemisphere 28, 29

plants 6, 12, 15, 17, 29
puddles 7, 13

rain 9, 12–13, 15, 19, 24
rainbows 7, 14–15

seasons 28–29
showers 12
sledding 7, 21
snow 9, 20–21
snowflakes 20
Southern Hemisphere 28, 29
spring 29
summer 28, 29
sun 8, 11, 14, 15, 16–17, 18, 26

thunderstorms 24–25

valleys 27

water cycle 18–19
water vapor 18, 19, 31
weather 7
winds 19, 24
winter 22, 29